Gardening

GARDENING AND THE LAW

The *Gardening Which?* guide to your legal rights in and around the garden

CONTENTS

INTRODUCTION

INTRODUCTION

Do you know what your legal rights are in the garden? Whether you've had problems buying plants, difficulties with neighbours or you've experienced poor service from a contractor, we can tell you where you stand. *Gardening Which?* hears from many members who have been sold faulty goods or poor quality plants. Companies that refuse to refund or replace these may be breaking the law and on pages 4-12 we tell you what you can do.

We have also heard many distressing tales about problems with neighbours and how relatively small boundary disputes can escalate into bitter arguments that smoulder on for years. The top ten causes of disputes are covered in this booklet with suggestions on how they are best tackled. Of course, the first step in any disagreement is to try to talk the problem through with your neighbour and see if there isn't a compromise solution. Often this is all that is necessary to repair neighbourly relations. However, if you cannot find a satisfactory solution, this booklet informs you of what your legal rights are and explains exactly what you can do to put things right.

If you are having trouble with your neighbours, try contacting Mediation UK, 82a Gloucester Road, Bishopston, Bristol BS7 8BW. ☎ (0117) 9241234.

They can put you in touch with a free local mediation service in your area, which may be able to help you resolve your dispute without the need to go to court.

SHOPPING FOR PLANTS

'The roses I bought by mail order weren't the colour stated in the advert'

see page 12

'A weed fork I bought from a garden centre broke the first time I used it'

see page 8

'They didn't tell me the *Pieris* I bought would only grow on acid soil'

see page 10

'The hedging plants looked half dead when they arrived and didn't survive their first winter'

see page 6

AND PRODUCTS

'When I got the coldframe home, there were no instructions and half the bits were missing'

see page 8

'I ordered red currants and got white currants instead!'

see page 10

'The advertisement said it would grow in shade, but I've since found out it needs full sun'

see page 12

'The tulip bulbs were soft and mouldy when I took them out of the packet'

see page 10

COMPLAINING ABOUT MAIL-ORDER PLANTS

Buying plants by post can save hours of fruitless searching at garden centres. But what if the plants you receive are dead on arrival, or turn out to be completely different from the ones described in the brochure?

What are your rights?

There are three main requirements under the Sale of Goods Act 1979 (as amended by the Sale and Supply of Goods Act 1994). If your plants and seeds don't meet these, you are entitled to a full refund, if you act quickly.

● Plants must be 'as described'. For example, if you buy a red rose which turns out to be yellow, you can return it and demand a refund.

● Plants must be of 'satisfactory quality'. This means the plants would be satisfactory to a reasonable person, taking into account the price and any description given to them, as well as any other relevant factors, such as the time of year. If the mail-order plants arrive with branches or lots of leaves missing or broken off, you could ask for a refund.

● Finally, they must be 'fit for their purpose'. For example, if plants have special requirements, such as an acid soil, and this was not made clear in the catalogue or advertisement, you could claim compensation.

The key to making a successful claim

If you are dissatisfied with mail-order plants, act quickly. Check the plants when they arrive and note any which you feel are below standard, taking photographs as evidence. If there is a problem, contact the retailer immediately. Keep a written, dated record of correspondence and conversations.

Making a complaint

In your letter, state exactly what the problem is and why you are dissatisfied. Emphasise your rights under the Sale of Goods Act (as amended). Tell the supplier whether you would like a refund or a replacement plant; you don't have to accept a replacement, if you would prefer a refund. Where possible, show what is wrong by returning the plant or sending photographs. If you wish to claim compensation for sundries, such as wasted compost, explain the reason.

If you are unsuccessful

Try contacting a more senior person in the company who has authority to make decisions. If you still don't succeed, you can pursue the matter through the small claims court. This covers claims of up to £3,000 in England and Wales, £1,000 in Northern Ireland and £750 in Scotland. You do not need a solicitor and it costs a maximum of £70 in England and Wales (fees vary in Scotland and Northern Ireland) to issue a summons. Ask at your local Citizens Advice Bureau or county court for details.

If you've been sold sub-standard plants or products, it's well worth persisting; *Gardening Which?* has found that nine out of ten complaints get successful results.

TAKING FAULTY GOODS BACK

Companies which refuse to refund faulty goods which are returned within a reasonable time of purchase are breaking the law, and you have every right to demand redress.

What are your rights?
If you have been sold faulty goods, you can take them back, under the terms of the Sale of Goods Act 1979 (as amended). This Act has three main points:

● Goods must be 'as described', so they must have the attributes detailed on packaging or at the point of sale.
● Goods must be 'of satisfactory quality', which means they must be in good condition, free from minor and major defects, durable, safe and able to do the job expected. For example, if you bought a shredder which blocks up every time you used it, it's clearly not 'of satisfactory quality'.
● Goods must be 'fit for their purpose'. If a water feature you bought constantly leaks, it is not acceptable.

If any of these terms are breached, you are entitled to your money back and possibly compensation, too. You are also entitled to examine goods properly before you lose your right to reject them; if you bought the shredder in winter and did not use it until spring, your rights would still be valid.

The key to making a successful claim

Firstly, before you buy a product, look at the instructions and ask for a demonstration, to check that it's what you need. Always keep receipts of goods you buy until you are sure they will be satisfactory. If you're not satisfied, contact the retailer as promptly as possible and keep a written, dated record of correspondence and conversations.

Making a complaint

Explain clearly what the problem is and give evidence, stating whether you want a full refund or a replacement product (you are not obliged to accept a replacement). Describe how you used the goods and, if you can, return the product or send photographs to show what went wrong. If your case merits compensation for extra costs incurred, explain what you wish to claim for and why.

If you are unsuccessful

Write to a more senior person in the company. If this approach fails, you can pursue the matter through the small claims court. This covers claims of up to £3,000 in England and Wales, £1,000 in Northern Ireland and £750 in Scotland. You do not need to use a solicitor and it costs a maximum of £70 (fees vary in Scotland and Northern Ireland) to issue a summons. Ask your Citizens Advice Bureau or county court for details.

   If you have been sold goods which are faulty, it is worth persisting with your claim. You have every right to a refund provided you return them within a reasonable time of purchase. Remember, the law is on your side.

TAKING PROBLEM PLANTS BACK

If you buy just the plant you've been looking for at the garden centre or nursery and it fails to thrive, despite the right growing conditions, what action can you take to resolve the problem?

What are your rights?
Members of the Garden Centre Association will take back plants with which customers are not satisfied during the first year after purchase. But should you run into problems, retailers must meet these three legal requirements of the Sale of Goods Act 1979 (as amended):

● Plants must be 'as described'; if you buy a purple lilac which turns out white, you have a right to take it back.
● Plants must be of 'satisfactory quality'. That is, what a reasonable person would expect, given the price and any other relevant factors such as time of year and pot size.
● Plants must be 'fit for their purpose'. For example, if it is not made clear to you when you buy a plant that it has special requirements – such as a lime-hating *Pieris* – you can claim a refund.

You are also entitled to examine plants properly before you lose your right to reject them. So, if you have to wait several months for a plant to flower before you realise it's the wrong colour, you should still be able to take it back.

The key to making a successful claim
If you visit a garden centre, check before you buy that a plant will meet your requirements. When you buy a plant, keep the receipt until you are sure it is satisfactory. If it is not, contact the retailer immediately and keep a written, dated record of correspondence and conversations.

Making a complaint
Explain clearly what the problem is and give evidence, explaining how you cared for the plants and, where possible, showing what went wrong by returning the plant or producing photographs. Tell the manager whether you want a full refund or a replacement plant (you are not obliged to accept a replacement). If you wish to claim compensation for sundries such as wasted compost, explain the reason why.

If you are unsuccessful
Contact a more senior person in the company. If you still don't get results, it may be worth pursuing a claim regarding expensive plants or a large order through the small claims court. This covers claims of up to £3,000 in England and Wales, £1,000 in Northern Ireland and £750 in Scotland. You do not need to use a solicitor and it costs a maximum of £70 (fees vary in Scotland and Northern Ireland) to issue a summons. Ask your local Citizens Advice Bureau or a county court for details.

MISLEADING ADVERTISEMENTS

Many gardening catalogues have sumptuous pictures of plants to entice you into buying. However, what happens when the plant turns out to be not only of poor quality, but not the plant it was claimed to be in the first place?

Complaints about advertisements regularly cite misleading descriptions, such as claims that a plant is rare to justify charging an exorbitant price. Photographs are also used to give a false impression of what to expect; montages are used, or the depiction of plants is exaggerated when colours are printed as stronger or brighter than they appear in reality.

What are your rights?

The Trade Descriptions Act 1968 makes it a criminal offence for traders to make false statements about the goods they sell. If you believe a trader is making a false claim, you should complain to your local Trading Standards Officer. They should investigate the complaint and, if necessary, take the trader to court if they think the Act has been breached. However, they cannot pursue any claim on your behalf for compensation suffered as a result of a misleading description.

To obtain a refund or compensation, you need to invoke the Sale of Goods Act 1979 (as amended) which requires that goods are 'as described', 'of satisfactory quality' and 'fit for their purpose'. If you wish to complain, keep a copy of the advertisement, a receipt for the goods bought and evidence of what went wrong. (For more detailed advice on making a successful claim, see 'Complaining about mail-order plants', page 6.)

Making a complaint about an advertisement

If you feel you'd like to take action to have a misleading advertisement withdrawn, you could make a complaint to the Advertising Standards Authority (ASA), which checks that advertisements abide by the British Code of Advertising Practice; this requires them to be 'legal, decent, honest and truthful'. If a complaint is made, the ASA will investigate the advertisement concerned. If they find it to be misleading, they can request that the company alter or withdraw the advertisement. Although they are not obliged to, most advertisers will act on the ASA's requests.

There is also a scheme called the Mail Order Protection Scheme (MOPS). It refunds customers who send money in response to 'cash with order' advertisements, and then lose it if the company goes bankrupt before the goods arrive. This service applies only to advertisements in national newspapers. However, readers of magazines which belong to the Periodical Publishers Association are covered by a similar scheme regarding mail order.

It's also worth writing to the advertising manager of the publication, outlining why you think it has carried a misleading advertisement.

PROBLEMS WITH YOUR

❝Weed seeds blow in from a neighbouring plot that's completely left to go wild❞
see page 16

❝Their front garden is full of rubbish and I'm worried about it attracting rats❞
see page 17

It's good to talk...
Before making a complaint, try to talk the problem through with your neighbour and see if there isn't a solution you are both happy with. Often simply a compromise is all that is necessary to repair neighbourly relations.

NEIGHBOURS

❝My new neighbours have their radio on full blast in the garden every weekend❞
see page 24

❝I'm fed up with my neighbour's cat digging up my garden and using it as a toilet❞
see page 28

...but if the talking stops

If you find talks with your neighbour reach an impasse, don't give up. You could try a mediation service – Mediation UK offers a free service in many areas and can be contacted on (0117) 924 1234.

WEEDS AND UNTIDY GARDENS

If you have a neglected garden near to your house that is a constant source of wind-blown weed seeds, what can you do? Does the owner of the land have responsibility for maintaining it? And, if so, what can you do to enforce it?

Talk to your neighbour
Weeds invading from nearby land or neglected gardens can be a constant source of annoyance for a keen gardener. However, see if you can find out why a garden has been left untended. Try to talk to your neighbours amicably. If

---

Weeds that must be controlled by law
The following weeds are defined as injurious in the Weeds Act 1959:
- Spear thistle (*Cirsium vulgare*)
- Creeping or field thistle (*Cirsium arvense*)
- Curled dock (*Rumex crispus*)
- Broad-leaved dock (*Rumex obtusifolius*)
- Ragwort (*Senecio jacobea*)

The Wildlife and Countryside Act 1981 makes it an offence to plant or cause to grow in the wild:
- Japanese knotweed (*Polygonum cuspidatum*)
- Giant hogweed (*Heracleum mantegazzianum*)

---

they are elderly and cannot cope with weeds, an offer of help may solve the problem. Even if the owner is busy or simply not interested in their garden, a few words of advice and encouragement may trigger appropriate action.

Weeds

The Weeds Act 1959 lists certain weeds (see Box, opposite) which are considered injurious and which the occupier of the land is legally obliged to control. The Act allows Ministry of Agriculture, Fisheries and Food (MAFF) officers to inspect any area suspected of harbouring these weeds. A written notice can then be served requiring the owner to prevent the weeds from spreading. If they fail to comply, they may be fined up to £1000.

If the problem is 'disturbing your enjoyment of your property' it might amount to a nuisance and you might be able to get an order served on the owners of the neglected land to prevent the weeds spreading, through the Environmental Health Department of your local council.

Weed-free zone

If all your attempts to prevent weeds spreading from neighbouring land fail, all you can do is make your garden as weed-resistant as possible. If creeping weeds, such as creeping thistles and ground elder, are the problem, you can prevent them spreading into your garden by sinking a barrier 15cm (6in) into the ground along the boundary.

Some weeds can be controlled with weedkiller. Ready-to-use glyphosate weedkiller sprays, for example, will knock back bindweed. Thick mulches of chipped bark will help prevent weed seeds from germinating. Otherwise, regular hoeing to keep weed seedlings from getting established is the only solution.

Piles of rubbish

There is no law which states that people must keep their gardens or land neat and tidy. However, you can take action if there is a health risk or if the mess is destroying the 'amenity' and the beauty of the neighbourhood.

This does not just mean neighbouring gardens. Where rubbish is an eyesore, the Town and Country Planning Act 1990 gives your local council the right to remove it. However, councils generally enforce the Act only in extreme circumstances. Petitioning local residents and presenting photographic evidence may well help your case.

If the rubbish is encouraging rats and mice, contact your local Environmental Health Department. They will then investigate and may serve notice requiring the removal of the rubbish if there is a proven risk to health due to vermin.

DO I HAVE A RIGHT TO LIGHT?

If the light in your garden is being blocked by a neighbour's hedge, trees or fence and a friendly word fails to improve matters, you may need to know where you stand legally and what action you can take.

What are your rights?
If tall hedges or trees are putting your garden in the shade, you can cut off any branches that overhang your side of the boundary. You can also prune back roots invading your property, even though this may put the offending plants at risk. You have to offer the branches or roots back to the neighbour, because they do not belong to you. However, you don't have the right to cut down vegetation on your neighbour's property or apply weedkiller to destroy the plants, however much shade they cast.

If you wish to do some pruning, check for tree preservation orders (TPOs) first.

Ask your local council (or the Department of the Environment, if you live in Northern Ireland) whether you need its consent first. If you live in a conservation area, it may want to put a preservation order on the tree. If it already has a preservation order on it and you prune it, you are committing an offence and could be fined.

The situation regarding fences and walls is that your neighbour can put up a fence or wall without planning permission as long as it's not over 1m (3ft3in) high where the land adjoins a road, path or pavement and not over 2m (6ft6in) where it joins your land. Any wall or fence higher than this needs permission.

Although not everyone has a right to light, it's worth checking your deeds, as some include a covenant which says your neighbours must not block out your light. Also, a covenant may forbid putting up fences or growing trees near a boundary. With 'open plan' housing estates, there may also be conditions attached to the land which prevent you putting up a fence, though usually just in the front garden. If you're in doubt, check with your local council.

If your garden has been cast in the shade, the law states that you can't force your neighbours to thin or reduce the height of their plants. You can acquire a right to light for a particular window in your house, or for a structure in your garden such as a greenhouse, but not for the garden itself.

With structures, the law states that if you have enjoyed a certain level of light for 20 uninterrupted years or more, you are entitled to expect a reasonable level of light in the future, though you can't insist on exactly the same amount of light that you have enjoyed in the past.

BOUNDARY DISPUTES

If a fence bordering your property needs repairing or replacing who should carry out the repairs? Is it the joint responsibility of both neighbours or does the boundary belong to one side? If so, how can you find out, and can you insist that the neighbour maintains their boundaries?

Who owns the fence?

To find out who owns the boundary of registered land, consult HM Land Registry (Land Register of Scotland). If the property is leasehold, look at the lease to find out who owns the boundaries. If the land is unregistered, examine the Title Deeds (your solicitor or mortgage lender should retain these). On the plan, there should be a small 'T' marked by the boundary. The side on which the 'T' is drawn indicates who owns the wall or fence. However, on its own the 'T' mark has no legal standing, so you need to check your deeds carefully for a written definition.

Who should maintain it?

There is no law that says fences should be maintained and hedges kept in trim. However, sometimes deeds state that the boundary must be kept in good repair or even replaced regularly. If no such clause exists, the owner is under no obligation to repair it. In practice, though, it's advisable to keep all fences in good repair as the owner is responsible for any damage or injury caused by neglected fences.

What if a boundary fence has been moved?

If the fence does not follow the line marked on the deeds, the original owner may have lost their right to move it back. In England, Wales and Northern Ireland you can become the owner of land through what is commonly known as 'squatters' rights' (technically called adverse possession). If you are using land which doesn't legally belong to you, but the true owner has done nothing about it for 12 years or more it becomes yours, as long as you have been using it without the real owner's permission. The only stipulation is that, during the period, you must have treated the land as your own. The most obvious proof that you are acting as the owner is to fence the area which you are claiming. Your claim is still valid even if the fence was put up or moved by a previous owner, provided the 12 years have elapsed since the fence was erected. If your land is registered, you can get your deeds changed to include the extra land. However, you cannot obtain ownership by adverse possession if you move the boundary and therefore trespass on your neighbour's land.

What about hedges?

A hedge that runs along a boundary line is usually the joint responsibility of both neighbours. In theory, you need your neighbour's agreement before trimming the hedge. If the hedge is just inside your neighbour's garden, they can ask to come round and trim it back. You are not obliged to allow neighbours access although, under the Access to Neighbouring Land Act 1992, they can apply to court for an order giving access to do the work. Your neighbour would have to make good any damage caused to your garden in the process. In this case, you have the right to trim any part of their hedge that encroaches over the boundary line, provided you offer to return the trimmings.

Pruning trees on the boundary

If a tree forms part of your boundary, do check for preservation orders before doing any pruning (see also 'Tree problems' page 36). Ask your local council (Department of the Environment in Northern Ireland). Similarly, if you live in a Conservation Area, you must tell your local council before you carry out any work on trees. It has six weeks to decide whether to put a tree preservation order (TPO) on the tree. Failure to comply with a TPO can result in fines of up to £20,000.

NOISY NEIGHBOURS

If the peace and tranquillity of your garden is shattered by thoughtless neighbours, is there anything you can do? How loud does a noise have to be to constitute a nuisance, and does it have to be a regular event before you can take action?

Talk to your neighbour

Everybody wants to live in peace with their neighbours, but people have different ideas about what constitutes anti-social noise. While a degree of tolerance is necessary, there is no need to suffer in silence. Try to talk to your neighbours amicably. If they are young they may be unaware that they are making sufficient noise to disturb their neighbours. If a breakdown in communication occurs, you could contact Mediation UK on (0117) 924 1234, which can put you in touch with a local mediation service.

Your rights

If diplomacy fails, the 1996 Noise Act gives householders more rights against unreasonably noisy neighbours who are disturbing them between 11pm and 7am. Environmental Health Officers (EHOs) will be able to measure the noise. If it exceeds a set level and a warning to be quiet is not heeded, they could then serve an on-the-spot penalty of £100.

Report intolerable or recurrent noise problems to your EHO. You'll probably be given a log sheet to record how and when the noise disturbs you.

It is a good idea to keep your own diary of disturbances too, and petitioning local residents for support will help your case. If it has affected your health, it's important to provide medical evidence.

If it is agreed that there is a problem, the EHO can serve a notice that specifies what the neighbours must do to cut down the noise. Failure to comply can mean a fine of £1000. The 1996 Noise Act also gives local authorities the right to confiscate noisy equipment.

Alternatively, you can go direct to the Magistrates' Court (the Sheriff's Court in Scotland). Again, you'll have a better chance of success if you can present documented evidence recorded over a period of time, and medical evidence if it has affected your health.

Garden machinery
Weekend relaxation in the garden can often be disturbed by daytime use of noisy machinery by neighbours. A recent *Gardening Which?* survey showed that the pitch of the sound is more important than the number of decibels produced. We are continuing our research into noise levels and hope to develop a rating system that will enable gardeners to choose the quietest and least irritating power tools.

NUISANCE FROM SMOKE AND SMELLS

Bonfires are one way of getting rid of garden rubbish that can't be composted, but they can also be anti-social. But does burning garden rubbish constitute a nuisance or pose a health risk to bystanders? If so, how regularly must it occur for there to be a legal solution?

How often can a neighbour light bonfires?
In general, there are no restrictions on when bonfires can be lit in the garden, though some councils do have by-laws which forbid the lighting of fires at stated times.

For bonfires to amount to a nuisance, you need to prove that they regularly interfere with your enjoyment of your property and that they are more frequent than an ordinary person would consider reasonable. For instance, if a neighbour regularly has bonfires when you usually sit in your garden or hang washing out, that could be deemed an unreasonable interference. Occasional bonfires, especially with prior warning, are unlikely to constitute a nuisance.

Who can I complain to?
If you are regularly bothered with smoke from neighbours' bonfires, you are entitled to complain to the local Environmental Health Department. If the Environmental Health Officer (EHO) judges the problem to be a statutory

nuisance, they may serve an abatement notice. Failure to comply with such a notice can lead to a fine of up to £5,000. Alternatively, you can apply to the Magistrates' Court for a nuisance order (Sheriff's Court if you live in Scotland).

The smoke produced by industry is strictly limited. Contact your local Environmental Health Officer if you are experiencing problems.

Other smokes and smells
Common garden smells such as a barbecue or a recently delivered pile of manure would not constitute a nuisance and are not worth taking action over. However, if the smell is from a leaking cesspit, unemptied dustbins or an industrial process, contact your local EHO.

PROBLEM PETS
AND ANIMALS

What can you do if a neighbour's pet uproots your prize chrysanthemums, digs its way under your fence or breaks your patio containers?

Initial steps

It is important not to let your emotions rule the day – don't get aggressive, no matter how great the damage. It's best to discuss the problem amicably and be sure that the neighbour's pet is the culprit. You'll also need to convince your neighbour that a problem exists. Ask them to visit your garden to see the damage and hopefully, empathise. Then, ask them to take steps to restrain the pet.

Pet deterrents

Dogs cause most problems in front gardens where there are no physical barriers to keep them out. The best you can do is hose down soiled plants to deter other dogs, and raise plants up in tall containers. In problem corners, think about replacing plants with rocks.

Cats are considered wild animals in the eyes of the law and they can wander where they wish. If you are troubled by cats soiling your garden, all you can do is use deterrents or mild scaring tactics. Minimise areas of bare soil or fine gravel, which may attract neighbourhood cats.

Taking legal action

If this doesn't work, you can resort to the law. Owners of domestic animals can be made liable for damage under the laws of trespass, though different rules apply to different animals.

If your neighbour's dog fouls your borders, thus damaging your property, for example, you will need to prove either that your neighbour failed to exercise reasonable control over the dog or that the owner actively encouraged their animal to damage your garden, in order to take action.

If, on the other hand, you are troubled by dogs which never stop barking, your local Environmental Health Department may be able to help. Contact the RSPCA if you have reason to suspect the animals are being neglected or mistreated. If you are threatened by aggressive dogs which could cause serious harm, phone the police.

Before bringing a case, make sure you have very good evidence. This means detailed records of times and incidents, statements from other neighbours and ideally photographs or video recordings of the offending animal in action and the damage caused.

Livestock

Farm animals such as cattle, sheep and horses can cause a lot of damage if they stray across your garden. The first step is to track down the owner, who will generally be held responsible for damage caused. Exceptions are mountain sheep, New Forest ponies and deer (other than those kept in an enclosed park).

What are your rights?

Where legal action is not warranted you have the following rights:

● You can remove or scare domestic animals from your land, including cats, but you mustn't use too much force. Spraying with water, shouting or throwing rotten fruit is about as far as you should go. You are breaking the law if you cause the animals any actual physical harm.

● If you are the boundary owner, it's up to you to block any possible entry points.

● Make sure your defences are safe; barbed wire or glass on top of walls, for example, may cause injury to pets and people, and you could be found responsible for injuries sustained.

● Animals that pose a health risk, such as rats or mice, can be dealt with by your local council. The Environmental Health Department could serve a notice requiring the removal of the rubbish that is attracting the vermin (see also page 18).

RIGHTS OF WAY

If your boundary wall needs essential maintenance, can your neighbours deny you access over their land? Or if you have a right of way over a neighbour's land (through a passageway, for example), but your neighbour makes access difficult because by blocking it with a car, is there anything you can do?

Access for maintenance
If you cross the boundary on to your neighbour's land without their permission you are trespassing. However, if your neighbour refuses you entry, you can apply to your local County Court (Sheriff's Court in Scotland) for permission for access. The Access to Neighbouring Land Act 1992 allows you to do this provided you can demonstrate that the work is necessary and can be completed only if you have access over your neighbour's land. You will have to 'make good' any damage caused during the maintenance and may have to pay a small sum to your neighbour for the access. If your house insurance does not cover you already, you may have to take out additional insurance to cover injury to bystanders and property before you start.

Blocked access

Where you have the right of way over a portion of your neighbour's land for access to your own garden, it will be set out clearly in the deeds of each property. In law, this is known as an easement (servitude in Scotland). Even if your neighbour has the right to park a car on the land, they cannot do it in such a way as to stop you exercising your rights of way. If they refuse to move the car, you could apply to the County Court for an 'injunction' (in Scotland apply to the Sheriff's Court for an 'interdict') to prevent your neighbour parking there. If they ignore an injunction they will be in contempt of court.

Public rights of way

Do you have a public right of way through your garden? Probably not, but are you sure? There are lots of examples of forgotten rights of way crossing private gardens. If a footpath is rediscovered and its existence is accepted by the local authority, you are obliged to keep it open for public access. If you are buying a house in the country, don't rely on maps or the deed of a property to prove whether there are any public rights of way. The only conclusive way is to contact your Highway Authority (usually the County Council). It will have what's called a 'Definitive Map and Statement' which shows and describes all rights of way. You are entitled to inspect this free of charge. The Authority should also have a Countryside Commission booklet entitled *A Guide to Definitive Map*

WHO'S RESPONSIBLE?

❝ If the paper boy falls on my uneven front path, could I be held responsible? ❞
see page 38

❝ Can my neighbours claim damages if my tree that overhangs their drive damages their car? ❞
see page 36

❝ If a contractor I hire has an accident, could I be sued for damages? ❞
see page 39

DISPOSING OF GARDEN CHEMICALS

Many gardeners end up with a stockpile of old garden chemicals in the shed, some of which may contain products which have since been banned. You are legally obliged to dispose of chemicals safely, but advice on how to do this can vary greatly. So what should you do?

Local authority services
Most local authorities request that chemicals are taken to the office at your local refuse or civic amenity site. What happens thereafter depends on the local authority. Many councils simply dispose of chemicals in landfill sites. Some, however, supply chemical cupboards at their refuse sites where chemicals are safely locked away until dealt with by a registered disposal company.

To find out about your local authority's disposal facilities, call your regional Environment Agency office or your local council's recycling and waste department. For details of your local civic amenity site, contact the waste disposal unit of your local authority or county council.

A few councils will arrange collection of unwanted chemicals, either for a fee or free of charge. Private waste disposal companies will also collect chemicals.

DIY disposal

If your council does not have good facilities for disposal of liquid chemicals, spray or pour them on to a gravel path or a bare patch of ground next to a shed or garage. Take care not to dispose of chemicals near ponds, ditches, marshes, streams or boundaries, and avoid places frequented by pets or other animals.

Don't pour garden chemicals down drains; some chemicals are extremely persistent and could find their way into streams and rivers where they may affect wildlife.

If you have small amounts of concentrated chemical, dilute as indicated on the label and dispose of as for liquid

chemicals. Very small amounts of solid chemical and empty containers can be thrown in the dustbin, but tighten the lids of containers first and wrap glass bottles in a newspaper.

Banned chemicals

It's worth checking labels for banned chemicals, such as those containing ioxynil or chlordane. For a list of banned chemicals, contact your regional Environment Agency, or your local MAFF office.

TREE PROBLEMS

A neighbour's overgrown tree can plunge your garden into shade, but can you demand they prune it? Your heavily laden fruit tree may well overhang your neighbour's garden, but how much of the fruit actually belongs to you?

What are your rights?

● A tree growing in your garden is your property and responsibility.

● Your tree's roots and branches can grow over into your neighbours' garden. However, your neighbour has the right to chop off these invading roots and branches where they cross the boundary.

● If you have a fruit tree that overhangs your neighbour's garden, any fruit it bears belongs to you, unless it falls naturally into your neighbour's garden, in which case the law assumes the fruit has been abandoned and belongs to your neighbour. Your neighbour cannot apply a poison to overhanging branches or roots that may kill the tree.

What if my tree causes damage?

● If you have trees in your garden, check that your insurance policy covers you for any damage they might cause, as you may be liable for the cost of putting things right. Diseased branches can fall off on to buildings, plants or even visitors to the garden. Tree roots can damage house foundations and lift paving.

● If your tree overhangs or obstructs a public footpath, the

local authority can order
it to be pruned or even
felled and send you the
bill. Electricity companies
have the same powers if a
tree interferes with their
supply lines.

● If the tree is in the
street, then it is the
responsibility of your
local authority.

● You are *not* responsible
for fallen leaves. A neighbour has no comeback if leaves
from your tree block his gutters or drains, for example.

Tree Preservation Orders

If you want to do any work on a tree in your garden check
with your local council to make sure it is not covered by a
Tree Preservation Order (TPO). This is an order imposed
by the local planning authority to protect trees in its area.
Even if you need to remove a dead branch, you must get
permission from your local authority. If it refuses, you
may appeal to the Department of the Environment within
28 days of your local authority objecting.

If you live in a Conservation Area, you have to tell your
local authority if you intend to do anything drastic to your
trees. The authority has six weeks in which to decide
whether to impose a TPO. Fines for ignoring a TPO or the
rules of a Conservation Area are very steep – up to
£20,000 for each tree and in some cases more.

PUBLIC LIABILITY

Unlikely as it may seem, if a visitor is injured while on your premises, they may be able to claim compensation from you. And visitors are not just invited friends – they include tradespeople, so it's important to know your rights.

Occupiers' liability
The Occupiers' Liability Act 1957 – in Scotland, the Occupiers' Liability [Scotland] Act 1960 – places a legal duty on occupiers of premises (owners or tenants) to see that all visitors are reasonably safe.

If, say, the milkman tripped on an uneven paving stone in your driveway which you knew, or should have known, needed repairing and broke his ankle, he might be able to prove that he sustained the injury as a result of your lack of care. You could then be responsible for paying compensation for the suffering caused (which could be substantial) and making up wages lost during the time the milkman has to take off work. If you have a wall or fence that, through neglect, falls and injures a third party or damages property you would be liable for damages.

Trees are a common cause for concern. A tree growing in your garden is your property and responsibility. It does not matter who planted it or if it was already there when you bought the land. If your tree causes damage, you may be liable for the cost of putting it right. Trees can cause damage in many ways. Diseased branches can fall off on to sheds or next door's house – worse still, onto visitors to your garden. Tree roots can damage house foundations, block drains or lift paving (see 'Tree problems', page 36).

Taking out insurance

It is very important that you have insurance to cover this kind of 'third party liability'. Your household insurance should include cover for this, so check carefully – most policies will cover you for £1 million. If you do face a claim, tell your insurance company immediately.

Hired help

Many house contents insurance policies cover your liability for domestic employees incase they have an accident on your property and claim damages for injury and loss suffered as a result. Contact your insurer to find out whether you are covered. You should point out dangers the gardener couldn't have reasonably been expected to know about – like electrical cables underground, or a disused well.

If any of your tools are used by the gardener, you must ensure that they are maintained safely. Lawnmowers and other power tools, for example, should be cleaned and serviced as required. You should also check that employees know about appropriate safety equipment to wear.

Self-employed professionals ought to have their own insurance. If a casual labourer calls at your house, ask whether they are insured before they start work.

How to complain effectively

If you have a complaint, it is important to register it quickly with the right person in the right way. Use the following action points to formalise your complaint.

Act quickly Go straight to the supplier as soon as you notice the problem or, if that is inconvenient, write.

Know your rights Read this booklet carefully before complaining so you know the legal basis of your claim.

Target your complaint Make sure you talk to someone in authority when you present your argument.

Keep a copy of all correspondence Keep a dated record of all contacts, whether written or verbal.

Put things in writing Unless the problem is solved immediately, make a complaint in writing.

● **Keep to the point** State the facts concisely so that your case is easy to understand and say what you want.

Keep evidence Record evidence clearly; keep invoices, catalogues, contract terms, advertisements etc.

Be persistent Don't be fobbed off with an excuse if you are not satisfied. A common excuse is 'we don't give refunds'. Notices saying 'no refunds' are against the law. Report any you see to your local Trading Standards Department. Other excuses include 'you're too late'; 'try the manufacturer'; 'you need a receipt'; 'no refunds on sale items'. These are all likely to be invalid if goods are faulty or unfit for their purpose.

Be reasonable Don't rule out compromise, as this can often be the best solution to the problem.

GETTING
JOBS DONE

❛What's the best way
to avoid employing
cowboy contractors for
garden maintenance?❜
see page 42

❛What if things
go wrong when
I've employed a
contractor?❜
see page 43

❛How can I
avoid being
overcharged
when having
my mower
serviced?❜
see page 45

EMPLOYING CONTRACTORS

When you can't do a job yourself, tales of rip-off cowboys make you wonder who you can trust. Following these steps should help you to get a job done well, at a fair price:

● **Know exactly what you want** Consult magazines, books and visit gardens to make firm decisions about what you want. Make notes and plans to show the tradesman.

● **Explain what you want** No contractor can do

a job that only you have in your head. Take time to discuss plans. Check that tasks are fully understood before giving the go-ahead. To minimise the risk of misunderstanding, put all the details in writing – use a straightforward written contract to establish what you expect from the contractor and what they expect from you (see also page 44). The contract should state your name and that of the contractor and should be signed by both parties.

● **Know the price is right** Don't agree that work may start unless you are happy with the price.

● **Check the credentials** If the job needs expertise, contact people the contractor has worked for in the past to check the quality of their work.

● **Keep redress as an option** Make sure you have the contractors name and address in case you want to get hold of them after the work is finished.

● **Pay on completion** Don't be talked into paying until the work is complete, in accordance with the contract and to a reasonable standard. Don't pay for materials up front.

● **If things go wrong** Write to the contractor immediately, stating why you aren't happy. If there is no reply after a week, send a second letter by recorded delivery. State that in the absence of a reply, you will hire another person to rectify the problem, and that the costs of this work will be recovered. If the contractor still fails to reply, or refuses to accept that the work is sub-standard, making a claim through the small claims court is your best bet. Photograph the sub-standard work and get an independent report from a third party, to be used as proof later on.

Getting insured

Many house contents insurance policies cover liability for domestic contractors. Contact your insurer to find out whether you are covered (see also 'Public liability', page 38).

The going rate

When getting someone to price a job, always ask for costs to be broken down, so you can compare like with like. You should always shop around – get at least three quotes.

1 I, _____ (**name of contractor**) of _____ shall carry out and complete the work outlined in the attached specification and drawings in a good, workmanlike manner in accordance with all relevant British Standards and Codes of Practice, all for the sum of £_____ **plus VAT** at the standard rate.

2 _____ (**name of contractor**) shall provide all the labour, materials and equipment necessary to complete the work.

3 The work shall start on [date]. The work shall be completed on [date]. Time is of the essence with regard to this work. The completion date will be extended only if the contractor is prevented from completing the work by factors outside his/her control. If the contractor, without good reason, fails to finish the work on time, s/he agrees to pay the owner damages which represent actual loss to the owner of £_____ for every week or part of a week during which the completion is delayed.

4 The contractor shall remove all rubbish as it accumulates, and all tools, surplus materials etc. from the site, and leave it in a clean and tidy condition within 14 days of completion of the contract.

5 The contractor shall comply with all statutory requirements, local and national regulations and by-laws that relate to the work. The contractor shall make all notifications, arrange inspections etc. in connection with the work. The contractor shall take out all the necessary insurance.

6 The terms and payment for any variation of the work should be agreed before it is carried out. Only variations authorised in writing by the owner shall be paid for.

7 If the contractor's work is not of a reasonable standard, or if the contractor leaves the site without reasonable explanation for more than four consecutive days, the owner may terminate the contract, paying only for the value of the work done, less compensation for inconvenience or additional expense, Seven days' written notice shall be given by either party to the other.

8 Once the contract is completed, the contractor shall submit a final account to the owner which is to be

MOWER SERVICING

You don't always get a thorough, safe service for your mower – the bill can be a nasty shock, too. However, not all agents are cowboys and you can take precautions to make sure you get value for money.

What can I expect my service to include?
A service can cost anything from £20 to £100, depending on the size and type of mower, but it is advisable to shop around for the best quote.

For electric mowers, a basic service should include:
● A check on all connections, switches, cords and insulation.
● A motor check.
● Blade sharpening or replacement (*see overleaf).

For a petrol mower there are eight checks which should be included in the service:
● An oil change
● Spark plug replaced

- Engine adjusted for easy starting
- Engine checked for efficient running
- Exhaust system checked
- Drive belt checked
- Blades sharpened[*]
- All cut-outs checked.

[*] for blade-sharpening expect to pay 50p-£2 per 2.5cm (1in) of blade

How to avoid being overcharged

Get a firm quote in writing beforehand. Make sure you get a quotation and not an estimate: an estimate is usually taken to be a provisional guide as to price, whereas a quotation is a fixed figure for the work to be done. You are obliged to pay only for work you have authorised. If the price has not been agreed beforehand, the law says you must pay a reasonable price – not necessarily what is demanded. Written quotes from other outlets are useful evidence of what is reasonable.

A repairer is entitled to hold on to your mower until you have paid what is legally due. So if you are forced to pay to get your mower back, make it clear in writing when you pay that you are paying under protest. This should protect your right to recover the excess later.

Always read the small print

Small print obliging you to pay promptly **is** legal – provided such terms were brought to your attention before

the work was carried out and you accepted them.

Any section of small print that restricts your statutory rights is not valid. Therefore, a phrase such as *'Any complaints must be made within 48 hours of delivery'* would be unfair, if you had not had a chance to examine the goods within the time specified. So if the claim went to court, this part of the agreement would be struck out.

What if I'm not satisfied with my service?

If, following its service, your mower fails to start or perform properly due to poor workmanship or faulty parts, the repairer may be in breach of contract. By law, you are entitled to claim for the cost of putting the faults right and any reasonable expenses you have incurred as a result.

Any damage done to the mower while it was on the repairer's premises is also their responsibility unless they can prove the damage was not their fault.

Before you make a claim, you need to give the repairer a chance to put things right. Take up any problems straight away, and if the problem is not resolved, write to the manager or owner explaining what you want done to rectify matters. You are entitled to a reasonable standard of services by virtue of the Supply of Goods and Services Act 1982 (in England, Wales and Northern Ireland). In Scotland, your rights are covered by common law.

HOW TO BECOME A MEMBER OF

Gardening
WHICH?

Gardening Which? is the ultimate gardening service.
Membership brings you:

- *Gardening Which?* magazine delivered to your door ten times a year
- FREE gardening advice by fax, e-mail or letter
- *Gardening Which?* OnHand – 24 hour advice on the telephone charged at the local rate
- Free seeds to try in your own garden
- FREE entry on weekdays to our gardens
- Discounts on our range of gardening books
- The chance to take part in our gardening trials

Gardening Which? is only available direct.
To try if FREE for three months, write to *Gardening Which?*
Dept C3896, Freepost, Hertford X, SG14 1YB or
FREEPHONE 0800 252 100 quoting C3896

Published by Which? Ltd
2 Marylebone Road
London NW1 4DF

First edition 1997
Reprinted July 1997, January 1998

Copyright © 1997 Which? Ltd

ISBN 0 85202 680 3

Cover design by Creation Communications

Compiled and edited by Jonathan Edwards, Martyn Hocking, Kate Hawkins and Hetty Don. Legal advice from Eileen Brennan and Jackie Hewitt

Printed by Bath Colour Press
Reprinted by GSM Ltd, Swindon